Masonic Meditations
Vol. 1

Symbols

Edited and Compiled by

RaMen

Authored by Dr. Jeff Menzise, 32°

Masonic Meditations Vol 1 - Symbols

10 9 8 7 6 5 4 3 2 1

Cover Artwork & Design by Jeffery Menzise, Ph.D. for Mind on the Matter Publishing

Library of Congress Cataloging-in-Publication Data
Menzise, Jeffery,
        Masonic Meditations Vol 1 - Symbols/ by Jeff Menzise, Ph.D.
includes Preface, Cover Artwork, & Design

ISBN: 978-0-9856657-2-2

Published in 2019 by
Mind on the Matter Publishing,
PO BOX 755, College Park, MD 20741
Website: www.mindonthematter.com
Email: drjeff@mindonthematter.com
Instagram & Twitter: @drjeffmenzise
Office Phone: 240-988-9639

Dedication

This book is dedicated to those truth seekers who journey through life seeking the answers to the questions that puzzle us all. I hope this series provides you with inspiration, insight, a thought-provoking exchange, and perhaps, a few answers.

Acknowledgment

We would like to thank the Phylaxis Society, the Phylaxis Magazine, Lux e Tenebris, as well as the Masonic Digest (published out of the Most Worshipful Prince Hall Grand Lodge of the District of Columbia) for originally publishing many of my thoughts shared in this series. We would also like to thank those who have requested a collection of Masonic writings authored by Dr. Jeff Menzise. We hope this response is sufficient.

Preface

This series presents an introductory view of my thoughts as both an initiate of several African spiritual systems, and an initiate up to the 32nd degree of the Scottish Rite and 10th degree of the York Rite, Prince Hall Freemasonry. The purpose for writing and now compiling this series is simply to offer an opinion and perspective on matters related to Freemasonry. The views that I provide are original but not necessarily unique, meaning, you may find similar statements shared by other Masonic and non-Masonic philosophers, authors, and scholars. The originality is in how I express these thoughts from my unique perspective having studied various philosophical systems, including the science of clinical psychology.

This three volume series is divided into the following subjects: Symbolism, Philosophy, and The Work. As a symbolist, I often seek the deeper meaning of both form and function; this is the theme running through volume one. Because Freemasonry is largely based on the symbolic form of communication, it has served as a field rich in resources for me to interpret and translate. The main feature of volume two, on philosophy, is a deep-dive into my views on the origins of Freemasonry as a system of human development. Finally, in volume three, I explore how the science of meditation and self-reflection is beneficial to Freemasons, within the context of our Craft.

There is something for everyone in this series. The wisdom and insights offered are universal and easily adapted to any existing religious and philosophical system or orientation. The practical tools offered alongside the cognitive exercise of reading each of the articles, is enough to form a new perspective for those who choose to engage the text on a deeper level.

Contents & Articles

An African-centered Perspective on the Definition of Freemasonry

Jeff Menzise, Ph.D., 32°, FPS

*A*s with all things in our Craft, the definition of Freemasonry is itself symbolically expressed. We use the symbolism of cryptic words and concepts to construct a sometimes-obscure statement regarding Freemasonry, what it is, and what it does. As part of my journey "Seeking More Light," I have looked deeper into our common, ritual-based definition of Freemasonry, and have sought to translate it by defining each individual word, forming a more detailed statement and explanation.

Many teachers have advised me over the years to always look up words you do not understand while reading. One suggested to stop reading as soon as you encounter such a word, and immediately look up its definition.

Mr. Neely Fuller, Jr. speaks on why it is important to ask others to define the terms they are using while conversing. This is a very practical means of minimizing confusion while interacting, and thereby increasing the chances of both parties walking away with a clear understanding of what was communicated.

For example, people will often ask for your religious affiliation with one of the following questions: "Are you a Christian?" or "Are you a Muslim?" Whenever I am confronted with such a question, my immediate response is always "Can you please tell me what you mean by 'Christian' (or 'Muslim')?" I do this because many times, people have entirely different definitions and understandings of the subject. Suppose a person who asks if I am a Muslim, defines a Muslim as "one who hates all people who are not Muslims." And let's say my definition is "one who submits to the Will of God." If I answer in the affirmative, based on my definition, in their minds, I have just admitted to hating all people who are not Muslims. The same is true with Christianity. If someone defines it as "a person who follows the Bible and has confessed their love for Jesus," and another defines it as "a white supremacist organization used to control the world," these two may be involved in the same conversation, but will be talking about two totally different things.

I only use the above examples to highlight the importance of taking time to define terms. When watching the movie *Malcolm X*, produced and directed by Spike Lee, I was exposed, for the first time, to the benefits of reading a dictionary. When I decided to do this for myself, I was amazed at the number of definitions each word carries. The word "start," for example, is typically used to mean "begin or initiate." However, later definitions will tell you that the word means "to protrude" or even "to give a sudden, involuntary jerk, jump, or twitch, as from a shock of surprise, alarm, or pain," as in to "startle."

I was totally intrigued by what I

learned by simply reading a dictionary. After meditating on the ritual definition of Freemasonry, I decided to apply this approach in order to gain a deeper understanding of the Craft. I literally took each word in the definition and analyzed all of them using their various definitions. In this manner, I came up with the expanded definition presented below. Keep in mind that this meditation is a working tool. As such, I recommend that you do what I did: look up the definitions for the following words: *peculiar, system, morality, veiled, allegory, illustrated (illustration)*, and *symbol*. This will prove to be a most fruitful and enlightening exercise for the Masonic Mind.

Read and think about the following expanded translation of the ritual definition of Freemasonry. Take some time to reflect on the individual statements. Seek to understand the deeper meaning of the words, and how they impact the way you understand, teach, and live Freemasonry. As descendants of the African Lodge, Prince Hall Masons should find this deciphering to be deeply refreshing, and surprisingly beneficial to their quest for "more Light." This holistic and inclusive approach to defining Freemasonry is much closer to our African worldview, than a superficial and cursory reading of the statement.

<u>The Ritual Definition:</u>

Freemasonry is a peculiar system of morality veiled in allegory and illustrated by symbols.

<u>The Ritual Definition expanded:</u>

Freemasonry is a distinguished adherence to Wisdom designed to align the aspirant with the Will and Power of the Supreme Being, thereby freeing them from the fetters of enslavement. It is identifiable by its ordered progression from one degree to the next, and is supremely exemplified in its interdependent structure of officers (with their respective stations), lectures, signs, passwords, and obligations. It is based upon the science of awakening and developing the innate divinity found within each human. The code of conduct, values, and practices are directly linked with the time proven processes maintained by the initiates of the highest orders of ancient times, and is exemplified by the various Volumes of Sacred Law. The "secrecy," or slight obstruction of Light, is not to conceal it from the non-initiat-

ed, but to protect both the Light bearer and the profane onlooker from being harmed; the former by ignorant zealots fearful of what they do not understand, and the latter by looking too deeply, too soon, at the tremendous nature of Light. The obstruction is usually translucent, allowing just enough Light to pass through, in order to pique and motivate the interest of those Seekers who have yet to intentionally embark upon their path towards enlightenment. The Light is regularly disseminated via palatable story chunks and ritual dramas, concealed from the profane by its apparently unrelated nature to the lessons it thus imparts. The key to unlocking this hidden Wisdom, is found by the earnest efforts of the initiate towards the cultivation of the necessary conditions of their own vehicles (body, mind, and soul). In true complementary fashion, Freemasonry shines Light onto seemingly obscure and abstract representations, in order to render them visible, comprehensible and practical to the aspirant. The true and living Word is the highest example and manifestation of Universal Truth, and thus, shining Light on the same, constitutes the methods used by Initiates of the highest Order. Symbols are used, in any initiation system, to train the mind of the initiate to develop the higher order thinking, discernment, and insight necessary to actualize the potentials purported

by our Craft and the processes thereof. The use of symbols both conceals and reveals the Light to Seekers, according to their degree of devotion to the process.

The above expanded definition should be read, and reread by those interested in developing a comprehensive understanding of what we are charged with as Freemasons. Contemplating this expanded definition will also assist those non-Masons to better understand Freemasonry as an organization and process. If we took this definition as our guiding Light, I'm pretty sure we'd be more intentional about how we travel.

Boston March 6. 1779

	Fellow Craft	Masters
worthey and amabell		Masters John Gish
	Allen Croft	Masters
Forbs	Cyrus Forbs	Prince Hall
Bristal Slincer	Bristal Slone	Thos... Dorrowicco
Saunderson	Thos Saunderson	Prince Saylor Mad... May 30
nee Saylor	Prince Saylor	Bristal Slone Mad... May 30
Nix Well	Nix Wells Decest this Life	Cyrus Forbs June the 2
ton Howard	ton Howard	Peter Best Mud... June 20 Decest
Prince Reed	Peter Freeman Decest this life	
tis Gill	Prince Reed	
Freeman		ton Howard May 4
iamn		
Buffom	Luke Belchard	Luke Belchard May 28
Belchard		
Met June 23 1779	Lanchester Hill	Lanchester Hill June 23
Woodman	Quintes Gill	Treasurey
Means	Boston Smith	Prince Reed June 23
Grigeory	Serar fleet	
Hill	Jube Hill	
day	Daniel Beale	Jube Hill January 26
	Beale underwoodman	
Spooner	William Gregeory	
letter	Means	Maj Bey...
	1792	W Hill Grigeo
	Nidleton	Quensey
	Sivea...	Essex

Initial Meditations, Thoughts, Questions, and Future Research Directions Regarding the March 6, 1778 Document

Jeff Menzise, Ph.D., 32°, FPS

I am thankful to Past Master Alton G. Roundtree for the opportunity to participate in this discussion on such an important topic. I have had this document in my possession since the early stages of research for my book Symbolically Speaking, vol. 1, but never had I explored this particular piece of history in depth nor to any degree of significance. Brother Roundtree contacted me and asked if I could render the image more readable and perhaps create a format that would facilitate printing a larger sized poster/

document for viewing at the Conference of Grand Masters, where he was to present his views and perspectives on the founding date for Prince Hall Freemasonry, then called African Lodge. I was glad to help. Upon completing the task, PM Roundtree mentioned possibly writing a brief article on the conclusiveness of the finding in order to bring the information to the Phylaxis Society and the readers of the Phylaxis Magazine. I agreed it would be a good idea and offered to co-author an article or to at-least contribute to the discussion. He was amenable to both suggestions.

Being the type of researcher and scholar that I am, I began to look through the document more closely and sought to further analyze the data. As I read through the handwritten archive, my forensic training kicked in, raising deeper questions about what I was seeing. The following are a few points of observation that will hopefully inspire this and future generations of masonic researchers to delve more deeply into the question of the origins of African Lodge #459, seeking to better understand what actually occurred, and where necessary, correct the existing historical record.

The Observations

- Prince Hall is listed as "Grand Master" with no visible date and month but with the year of 1778. Some of the other Brothers in the "Master Mason" column are clearly declared "Maid Master" next to their names. This points out the possibility that something different occurred with Prince Hall than with the other Brothers, and also confirms that Prince Hall officially carried the title "Grand Master." This seems to indicate that Prince Hall was actually raised at an earlier date, and made "Grand Master" in 1778.
- The earliest visible date and month for the Master Masons listed is May 30, 1778.
- Some of the dates for the "making" of Master Masons extend into at least 1779, but probably at least into 1780, citing Jube Hill's "Master Mason" entry as an example (dated January 26 with no year, after Prince Reed's June 23,

1779 entry). There also seems to be a 1782 date entered under the Fellow Craft column for an unknown Brother (name is illegible).

- Brother Petter Betts is listed as "Decest [deceased] this Life" in both the Fellow Craft and Master Mason column (dated June 20 177?). Peter Freeman is also listed as "Decest [deceased] this Life" in the Fellow Craft column. This fact, along with others previously and still to be cited, makes it likely that this document is a transcription of information from another record; perhaps an original ledger.

- There are discrepancies regarding the spelling of certain names, some of which are significant to the point of being a name close to the ones we usually use, but are different altogether. For example, there is a Brother listed as "Prince Taylor" that may be the name "Prince Rayden" that I have seen used as one of the "Founding 15." Another example is "Petter Betts" as listed on the document could be the Peter Best that some list as a member of the

"Founding 15." There are several other examples found in this document.

- All 14 of the Brothers reported to have been initiated with Prince Hall do not all appear under the Master Mason column of this document. Additionally, "Fortin Howard," one of the "Founding 15" is actually listed as being raised on May 14, 1779, indicating that not everyone in the "Founding 15" were initiated, passed, and raised, at the same time. "Prince Reed" (Rees) is listed as being raised on June 23, 1779. My understanding of what John Batts originally did with the "Founding 15" is that he initiated and maybe even passed some of them, but not make Master Masons of all of them at the original ceremony. This may be the reason for a discrepancy in when African Lodge #1 (or Prince Hall Freemasonry) actually began. It is possible that they were initiated, and maybe passed, in 1775 but actually not raised until 1778, giving them the ability to form a Lodge at this time, having at least three Master Masons.

- There are Brothers "maid master" under the Master Mason column that DO NOT appear amongst the founding 15 with Prince Hall, namely: Lancaster Hill, Luke Belchard, Quentes Gill, Jube Hill, etc. While some of the "Founding 15" do not legibly appear in the Master Mason column.

Initial Thoughts – Summary

The fact that there appear dates from 1779 on a document headed March 6, 1778, raises questions regarding the authenticity of this record. I offer several explanations/hypotheses for this occurrence. One is that this is an actual page from a Ledger began on March 6, 1778 and simply continued on as Brothers were initiated, passed, and raised. If this explanation is true, then there must have been an earlier document that includes where Prince Hall himself was initiated, passed, and raised, because, as cited above, he only appears on this list as "Grand Master" in 1778, and nowhere else on the document as the other Brothers do.

Further, if this document were began in March of 1778, many of the Brothers would have to have either been "made at sight," or maybe initiated in March, and taking the subsequent degrees culminating in dates of raising spanning from May, 1778 (three months later) to possibly January, 1780.

There are still many questions to be considered and answered before we get to the bottom of the question of our origins as descendants of African Lodge #1. We have a lot of work ahead of us as we re-fortify the foundations of our Craft as Prince Hall Masons. This is the type of labor for which we should rejoice; thankful for having the opportunity to toil in the quarries and sift through the rubbish in search of our Master Key. Once found, we can use it to unlock the fullness of our inheritance, which is an honor without equal.

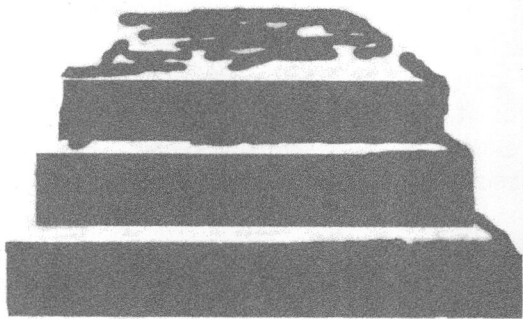

The Three Steps

Jeff Menzise, Ph.D., 32°, FPS

*O*ur Craft is steeped in symbolism and allegory, all of which have an infinite number of interpretations, designed to develop a deep, insightful, and practical understanding of life. As Freemasons, we are looked upon by society as the keepers of Light; we are thought to be those who carry on the traditions established by our most Ancient of Ancestors, the Grand Architect Of The Universe (GAOTU). Being the fashioner of all that is, the GAOTU must've fashioned all things according to the same laws that we seek and observe in our Lodge. This bit of fact means that everything is, in one way or another, directly related to our works, and thus can lend itself as a tool for the continued building of our Temple.

This being said, it would be beneficial to realize that we have unlimited access, via the Law of Analogy, to the deepest knowledge, wisdom, and understanding that this universe has to offer. Unfortunately, many have been trained to function in a very limited and rigid mode; acknowledging only those things that were handed to them by those who were a part of their Raising, without regard to the levels of consciousness of those doing the Raising. If, for example, I never sought to use the tools my high school teachers gave to me, in pursuit of more knowledge, I would forever have been limited to my high school education. Instead, I took the tools and applied them to the higher levels that remained in front of me. The same is true for my Masonic experience.

We were all given a set of keys. Some of us are satisfied with placing them in the trophy case and proudly displaying them to our guests and visitors. Others of us carry them around and randomly try various doors to see if they actually work and can be used in real life. Then there are those of us who know, beyond the shadow of any doubt, that the keys do work, that they are designed for actual locks, and thus, we use our time seeking to figure out which keys go to which locks, and then, actually using those keys to open them. Each group listed above is functioning according to their own will and desire, and thus, none of them are more correct or incorrect than the other. The difference amongst them is that some are collectors of trophies, others recognize they have tools but are not fully committed to using them, and finally, the last group acknowledges the tools, learns to use them, with the goal of mastery, which is eventually attained by applying the newly acquired knowledge and skills.

This point serves as a good segue into our topic for this article, *The Three Steps*. According to our <u>Standard Masonic Monitor</u>, *The Three Steps* are:

> Emblematical of the three principal stages of human life: Youth, Manhood and Age. In Youth, as Entered Apprentices, we ought industriously to occupy our minds in the attainment of useful knowledge; in Manhood, as Fellow Crafts, we should apply our knowledge to the discharge of our respective duties to God,

our neighbor and ourselves, so that in Age, as Master Masons, we may enjoy the happy reflection consequent on a well-spent life, and die in the hope of a glorious immortality.

The dissertation continues:

The Three Steps are also symbolical of the three stages of human progress. It is one of the most striking proofs of the infinite benevolence of the Deity that he has created man ignorant[1], but with

---

1   As a descendant of the African Lodge, I maintain an African-centered perspective of our Craft and its Symbols. I read the Monitor's explanation of the Three Steps and disagree with the statement that man is created in "total ignorance." Man is **not** created in "total" ignorance. The body is part of man, and is highly competent at all that it does, therefore, proving the statement untrue. Man's ignorance does not make us an ignorant creature by creation nor nature. Instead, Man is created in a receptive state as a function of the Law of Polarity. Thus, the human brain, mind, and body naturally absorb, learn, assimilate, and build based on what it is exposed to. Therefore, the total being of Man is designed to grow and develop from conception, and grows more skillful at this task, by acquiring and applying new understanding. On the flip side,

an unlimited capacity to learn, thereby placing within his reach those sublime enjoyments and enduring and satisfying pleasures which arise from the constant acquisition of knowledge. Man's nature is so constituted that his happiness consists in unceasing acquisition and perpetual progress...Here is a remarkable picture [referring to Alexander the Great] of the wretched and miserable creature man would be should he find a limit to his advancement or arrive at a period when nothing would remain for him to aspire to. But the objects of knowledge are infinite, and therefore the fountains of wisdom at which he may drink are inexhaustible.

This sublime truth, that man was created for eternal progress, was one of the earliest teachings of Freemasonry, and was illustrated in its most ancient rites. And to-day the Order announces it in multifarious forms and asserts it in all its instructions. Not only is it symbolized by the Three Steps, but it is the great and living thought that inspires the entire ritual.

Man is also highly skilled at countering and even stifling their own growth and development, making self-discipline and discernment a necessity.

Embedded in this explanation of the symbol are several guideposts, leading the astute Mason towards a deeper understanding of the various roles they will play in life, as well as the various stages he will go through. Before we begin to deepen our perspective of what is written in the *Monitor*, let us first explore the most obvious question: Why are there three steps?

The number three is a very significant symbol in many ancient traditions. According to *Sacred Geometry and the Science of Motion and Number*, the number three is symbolically represented by a perfect triangle. This triangle, if viewed as a dynamic and moving shape, becomes a tool for deepening our understanding of how the *Law of Opposites* and the *Law of Balance* operate in our day-to-day lives.

Picture, if you will, a spinning dot. Half of this dot is colored blue and the other half is red (see figure 1). This dot represents the joint force of electro-magnetism (red is electric; blue is magnetic). As the dot spins the electric and magnetic forces fly off in opposite directions, 180° on the Level (see figure 2). Both of these charges are positive in polarity (although they are opposite to each other ...electric is the "positive" pole to magnetism's "negative"), and thus seek a force that will draw them towards each other once again (see figure 3). Wherever this force is, it will surely draw the two in, causing them to form a new and complementary angle to the once 180° trajectory. Now this is really intriguing because, as we all know, EVERY triangle measures to be 180°, so no degrees are lost in the formation of the shape, it literally just changes form (this is analogous to Newton's Law of Conservation where energy is neither created nor destroyed; it only changes form and states).

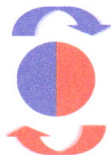

Figure 1.

Figure 2.

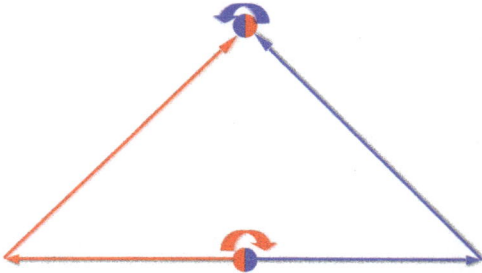

Figure 3.

The angle and style of triangle depends on the location of the complementary "negative" dot. If it is perpendicular to the original dot, it will form a 45°- 45°- 90° triangle or perhaps a 60° - 60° - 60° triangle, depending on the distance between the two dots. Move it to the left or right of the perpendicular, we would have a 30° - 60° - 90° triangle, and so forth. This understanding becomes useful in day-to-day living, once we identify the individual parts with variables in our social situations. Let's say the initial spinning dot represents the things we intentionally set in motion, seeking to buy a car for example. We put our energies and intent out into the world that that is what we are aiming to do (this is the electromagnetic energies being sent out from the dot). We must then have a focal point for this energy, else it will simply continue ad infinitum, eventually being pulled towards something that is not intended (energy could be diverted and distracted by using the money you are saving for a car on partying because now you "have the money" to do it).

As Master of "our Fate," and Captain of "our Souls," we intentionally place the focal point ("negative" dot) where we need or want it, thereby intentionally drawing the energies (electric/"positive" and magnetic/"negative") towards it (something that will make our desires and goals manifest efficiently and effectively). This could be something as simple as beginning to read about cars in magazines or online, etc. It could also be intentionally working to improve one's credit score for the purpose of improving a loan rate when purchasing your car. Subsequently, once the energy "circuit" is closed, the energy can now flow in a precise path, creating a specific shape, bringing about definite results.

This same science can be applied to all situations in life. If we take a look at many of the symbols of our Craft, we will see that many degrees use triangles. For example, my Companions (Royal Arch Masons) know that the red triangle, within the circle, carries three within it. Now those three separate symbols (the circle, triangle, and tau) are three levels of symbol, one of which is a triplicate. Embedded in this symbol is a hidden mathematical formula and truth demonstrating the number of degrees in a radian[2]. This is all based on the three.

We could go on for days talking about the threes that symbolize perfection, progress, balance, and completion. Recognizing the fact that we have three degrees in the Blue House, that there are three principle Lodge Officers, that there were three

2   A radian is a unit of measurement used when measuring an arc in relationship to the radius of a circle. One radian roughly translates into 57.296°.

Master Builders, that there were three Ruffians, and three parts to the third degree, with the Scottish Rite rising to the thirty-third degree, only begins to scratch the surface. Specifically to us, the descendants of the African Lodge, the number three also shows up in the three Founding Brothers with the first name "Prince." Are these the "Three Kings" in Youth form, destined to recognize and anoint the "Prince of Peace" at his birth; or are they better known as the three Magi (Magicians), who recognized an Eastern Star and interpreted the signs?

According to Pierson's *Traditions of Freemasonry*:

> The ternary [or triad] is the first of unequal numbers. The triad, mysterious number, which plays so great a part in the traditions of Asia, the philosophy of Plato, the mysteries of all ages, an image of the Supreme Being, includes in itself the properties of the two first numbers [1 + 2 = 3]. It was to philosophers the most excellent and favourite number, a mysterious type, revered by all antiquity and consecrated in the mysteries; wherefore there are but three essential degrees among Masons,

who venerate in the triangle the most august mystery—that of the Sacred Triad, object of their homage and study.

If we look at the three steps in relationship to taking paces (ambulating), we can unearth a very interesting message. Three steps in this regard, identify an intentional movement towards a goal. The first step could have been the result of a stumble or a sign of being off balance. The second step may simply be employed to recover balance. The third step, in many cases, is a continuation of the previous movement (steps one and two), and thus, represents intentionality. Thinking back to some of the first questions we are asked during our introduction into the Lodge, we know how important intentional and self-directed movements are. The third step commits you to the process.

Our Ancient Ancestors in the Nile Valley of North East Africa also symbolized the Three Steps. Their description seems to have influenced the version we find in the Monitor, or to have at least derived from the same source. In Kemet (Ancient Egypt), the steps were symbolized by the Sun at its three stages: Rising, Apex/Zenith ("The Most High"), and Setting (see figure 4). In its rising form, it was called Khepra, Herukhuti (Heru of the Horizons), Ra-Herukhuti or sometimes Heru-p-Khart (Heru the Child). It symbolized youth and a new day.

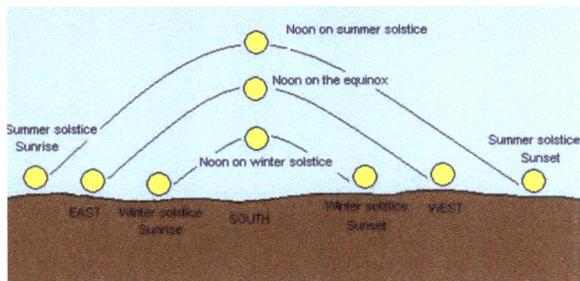

Figure 4. Three phases of the sun at three times of the year. (Image credit: http://facstaff.gpc.edu/~pgore/Earth&Space/GPS/motion_of_objects_in_sky.html)

The Sun at its zenith, known as "the most high" sun, was acknowledged as the most powerful place for the sun. It was sometimes called Ra or Heru Behdety (symbolized by a winged sun-disk...similar to the one found inside the Washington Monument rising above a sculpture of George Washington...see figure 5). This is the version of Heru (Man) that applied knowledge in order to gain spiritual enlightenment.

39

Figure 5. Heru Behdhet found in the Washington Monument. (Photo Credit: Jeff Menzise, Ph.D.)

Finally, Heru Ur (Heru the Elder) is the tried, tested, and ready to be tried again, setting sun. He wears the double-crown of both Upper and Lower Egypt, a symbol that demonstrates his ability to control his upper and lower natures, serving as Master of his Temple.

Speaking directly to the way the "Three Steps" are explained in the Monitor, we will also unearth some jewels that, if correctly applied, will greatly improve our Brotherhood and experiences in the Craft. Let's begin with the three life stages as outlined above: Youth, Adult, and Elder. Never before have I seen such an intergenerational fellowship as powerful and naturally connected as I find in the Lodge. We have Youth in the form of those that are literally younger in age, as well as those who are newly Raised Brethren.

We have the Adults, who are ideally making their rounds to each station, with more years in the Lodge and Life as well. Then we have our Elders; these are our collection of Past Masters and their equivalents in the other Houses; Brothers that have been in and served the Craft for decades, and/or in various positions.

According to the Monitor, the Youth are to best spend their time actively seeking and acquiring useful and beneficial knowledge. They are expected to be curious, interested, and excited about learning new and enriching information. The energy of youth makes this the most beneficial time for this to take place. Youthful energy is still in the growth phase (as demonstrated earlier), thus, it is more receptive, and better equipped for the assimilation of new information.

The Adults are fresh out of their information gathering phase and are most beneficial in the mode of making the information practical and actually showing and proving it's value by applying it to their own lives for others to witness and model. This is perfect for the Adult phase because energies are being redirected from the growth and receptive phase of Youth, towards the strengthening and balancing effects of Adulthood. The marvelous thing about these phases is that there are physical as well as mental attributes of each. On the physical level, the body begins to change in regards to the hormones produced and circulated, which in turn switches up how the body functions. Mentally, as adults, we begin to think more deeply about things and have a lot more life experiences against which to compare what we have learned in our previous phase.

The third step is that of being an Elder. Elders have a track record of showing and proving their knowledge. They are the one's who have lived long enough to actually Know many things about many things. They are fully capable of identifying and discerning information through the Law of Analogy. Their wisdom is made evident by their thoughts, speech, and action. They are the backbone of any society because they have lived the longest, and carry the living memories of yesterday. They have likely served all stations and thus, are capable of filling in for any one of them. They have been Brothers with more Brothers longer, and thus are amongst people with whom they have grown and learned.

When these three steps are understood and everyone celebrated in their role, a sort of powerful harmony is generated. For example, if the Youth of our Lodges are encouraged to seek Light for the purpose of bringing it back to the Lodge, they will be more connected with the Lodge based on having a purpose for being in the Lodge, as well as feeling good about being contributors to the Lodge beyond the paying of dues and the giving of time for meetings.

Many times, our "Youth" are viewed as people who have nothing to contribute and who are there to basically "learn the ropes." They are often relegated to an inferior status, and their energetic desire to "Seek More Light" is often dimmed by the Adults and Elders who have always done things a certain way, and thus, are not open or receptive to what the Youth may bring to the table. Now, there are boundaries and certain immoveables that must always be followed; however, there remains an IN-FINITE amount of knowledge and wisdom that can be sought and applied within these parameters.

Our Adults, respecting the Youth and the knowledge they bring forth, will be equally excited about trying out the new knowledge and showing and proving, fortifying or discarding it, depending on it's quality. These Adults are capable of being a fair judge of the Youth's Knowledge only because they too have spent their earlier days pursuing Knowledge and thus are Knowledgeable. The Adults, in their practical mode, begin to strengthen the foundations and pillars of the Lodge by constantly contributing to the growth and development of the Brothers therein. Each one, from their respective stations, plays a very specific role, and thus, is equipped to handle the knowledge in their own way.

For example, the WM has the responsibility of providing the space for the Youth to bring their knowledge and insight into the Lodge. He will set the tone and provide the example of how the rest of the Lodge is to respect what our Youth are bringing in. The WM is also responsible for guiding and demonstrating to the Youth how we should discern the information they are sifting through and how to present it in a way that is easily assimilated by the rest of the Lodge. The Adults validate the Youth, and are themselves supported by the strength of the Elders who stand behind them. Having this sure-footed support brings confidence into Brothers, and thus into the Lodge.

Having a group of well-respected Elders is just as important as having courageous Youth. These Elders, being honored by all others, will find themselves in a role where their wisdom is valued, and where their experiences, understanding, time served, and mastery are regarded with high esteem. This experience will breathe into them a degree of vitality that will increase the quality and length of their days here with us. Keeping our living history, living history.

The honored Elder is thus infused with a sense of accomplishment and Faith about the future of our Craft. The goal of the rest of the Lodge should be to make our Elders proud. To provide them with a sense of achievement and fulfillment by demonstrating that the Legacy that they helped create, will continue on strong, constantly improving and becoming more permanent in its Valor. Currently, many Elders are critical and dissatisfied with what they find in our Lodges. This is due, in part, to their lack of flexibility in regards to the need for us to continue learning, building, and creating our Craft to be the system it once was. The other part is the fact that we do not have a system that encourages a synergistic and complementary flow between the Three Steps. By looking at this situation as descendants of the African Lodge, we will find that it is directly in line with our Ancestral cultures. Elders are highly honored and revered for the very reasons outlined above. They form an Elite council within the village-community, making important decisions and bringing a Divine perspective to the conversation. Newborns and Elders are the closest groups to our Ancestors and God, a fact that increases and justifies their value.

In conclusion, the Three Steps, like our many other symbols, carry ever-deepening levels of Wisdom and insight that serves us well, if and when we translate and apply them to our purposes as Prince Hall Freemasons; descendants of the African Lodge. Our Lodges will continue to grow, flourish, and give birth to future generations of Masons. The time is now for us to determine what condition the Temple will be in when they arrive. It takes us all, working together...one step at a time.

On the Square

Jeff Menzise, Ph.D., 32°, FPS

*W*hat is more important for a Masonic Brother than to be ever on his square? It is the basic foundation upon which we are to govern our lives; ensuring that we measure our steps and weigh our words, that all angles are correct and that we maintain a particular posture both in public and in our private lives. We are most capable of living up to this lofty goal with the support of our fellow travelers who are both willing and able to extend the length of their cable-tows, within their honest means. This initial article, in an on-going series will provide a preview of the many ways that we are called to live our lives on the square. With each publication, we will be presented with practical advice detailing how we can consistently and intentionally firm up our square, and live up to our Masonic duties.

No man is an island. This truism is no more observable than within our Fraternal Order. The fact that it takes very specific numbers to open a lodge, conduct transactions, and perform our obligatory duties is evidence enough. We need each other. The strength and quality of our individual squares is what holds the foundation together: weakened and bent squares create curved and unstable lines, while straight and proven squares provide us with efficient and direct measurements with very little distraction and need for detour.

As nature leads. The process of being on our square should be easy and natural; each and every one of us that has been "regularly raised" from the dead level to that of the living perpendicular was done so on the square. When that final deathblow was dealt and all of our former fragile and mortal ways were rendered impotent, we were resurrected with a new nature, a renewed sense of self that is without the illusions of limitations that suffers the non-Mason. Thus, it is in our very nature to be great; the only difference between us and those who have not been initiated, passed, and raised is that we are sure of it and have the evidence to prove it.

To whom much is given, much is required. Being sure comes with its own cost and set of responsibilities. It means that when the pressure is on, we no longer have the luxury of crumbling under the force. It means that when emotions begin to flare, we are expected to be "Steadfast as the Sons of Steadfast, reigning from the land of Steadfastness." We no longer have recourse to the excuses that work for the normal person, but instead, we sympathize for those who still find comfort in their use. We look on with compassion and deep understanding, as a parent does a child who is still finding their way. We, in all humility, extend our prayers and well wishes that they too will one day seek and find their Light. In the meantime, we vow to relieve their burden in order that they may survive its weight.

Family first. While we have such lofty goals and positions in and for the community-at-large, we must remember that family and personal lives are not to suffer. For what good is it to receive accolades and praise in the streets and be scorned at home? Heavy is the heart of a man who has let his family down in service of the Lodge. Shameful is the look in the eyes of a Brother whose children have grown without their guidance because they were too busy jockeying for a position of authority amongst those who are forever and permanently equals. Irresponsible is the title given to the Brother who has financially burdened his home in order that he may be seen as a financial provider to the Lodge. To strike a healthy balance between family duties and Lodge obligation is a skill to be cultivated and cherished. The one who exemplifies this ability, should be held in high esteem and honored amongst his Bredren.

I look forward to sharing more light with my Brothers in a very practical and empowering way with every publication of the on-going article "On the Square." If there are certain and specific topics that you would like for me to address, or specific issues that one needs guidance on, please feel free to communicate this desire to me, and I will be sure to include it.

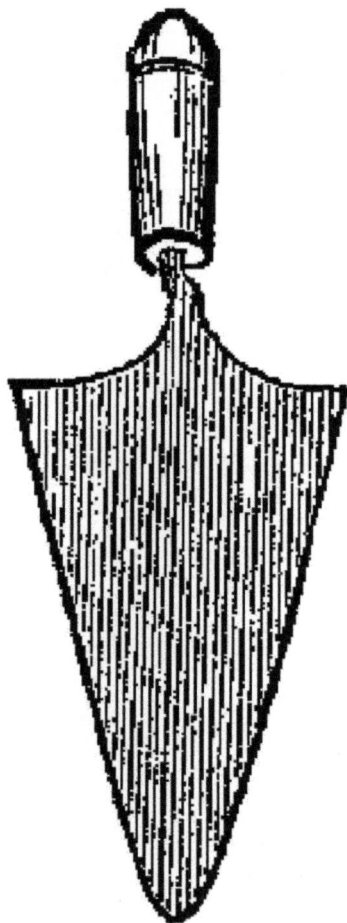

54

A 32ⁿᵈ Degree Meditation on the Trowel

Jeff Menzise, Ph.D., 32°, FPS

*I*n our Standard Monitor, we are told that all Masonic tools are the working tools of the Master Mason, "especially the Trowel." Simons continues:

> *The Trowel is an instrument used by operative masons to spread the cement which unites the building into one common mass; but we, as Free and Accepted Masons, are taught to use it for the more noble and glorious purpose of spreading the cement of brotherly love and affection—that cement which unites us into one sacred band or society of friends and brothers, among whom no contention should ever exist, save that noble contention, or rather emulation, of who best can work and best agree. – **p. 92**

Like the record breaking 8.1 magnitude earthquake that hit California at the

San Andreas fault, we can sometimes experience hardship and circumstances that not only impact us as individuals, but also the entire Prince Hall Masonic PHAmily; leaving us vulnerable to further injury. Experiencing internal turmoil, one can't help but to feel both disappointment and excitement. The disappointment is in response to the lack of "brotherly love" so often displayed when disagreements and misunderstandings arise. The excitement is in response to the great opportunities that become apparent, once the dust settles and we are able to see beyond our emotional discomfort and get back to work.

The lack of "brotherly love" is a symptom of our deeply repressed emotional trauma brought about by that death-blow that knocked us, descendants of African Lodge, unconscious when the Ruffians sought to steal our most prized and irreplaceable possession. This trauma has left us susceptible to in-fighting, which is itself, an outgrowth of underdeveloped men, claiming to be whole and mighty. This is the precise antithesis to what we have been taught about the Trowel. Those among us who are the Master Carpenters, the Master Joiners, the Master Welders, the Master Healers, the Master Brick Layers, the Master Concrete Pourers—in other words, the Master Masons who speculate operatively—typically see this as an exciting time, ripe with a Grand opportunity to correct an error in the structure of our Supreme monument, that was built and dedicated to the Sovereign nature of the truly God-Inspired man.

For those of us in the Consistory and beyond, in honor of our Royal blood, we must constantly refine our thoughts, our speech, and our actions to reflect the discipline required of a Sublime Prince. We must continually focus and train our eyes in order to objectively Inspect our works, shamelessly correcting the errors as soon as one is discovered, regardless of the cost, and regardless of whose work we are calling into question. We must finally remember that we are here to make Good Men Better. Sometimes this requires a precise and clean cut from the surgeon's scalpel, or perhaps the wielding of a jack hammer to break up a weak foundation, or maybe even an "act of God," in the form of a swift and unpredictable earthquake, sent to expose the heretofore unrecognized fault line, made volatile by the friction of two tectonic plates moving in opposite directions; fighting for the same territory, piece of land, or jurisdiction.

As Master Masons, we have been provided with every tool that we could possibly need, to remain a strong and healthy organization of Men. We have enough expertise, experience, insight, wisdom, and fortitude to weather any storm that may come our way. It is time for us to pull out our Trowels, start mixing our cement, and begin to spread what we know to be the most important underlying principle of our Craft: Love for Self, Love for Our Brothers, and Love for Our Organization. Without this, we will forever remain buried in the shallowest of graves; conscious only of our limitations, and frustrated by our impotence.

The Hour-Glass

Jeff Menzise, Ph.D., 32°, FPS

*F*ull of allegory and symbolism, our Craft is one that both intrigues and strikes the uninitiated with awe. The strangeness of a language that does not readily lend itself to common interpretation is perhaps the most beneficial way of protecting sacred wisdom, while simultaneously promoting the quest for "Light" outside of the Lodge. From the days of infancy, whether speaking of a newborn baby or a newly initiated E.A., the influx of new stimulation via the physical senses inspires the brain and mind to begin seeking answers. This quest has, as a natural part of it's process, the questioning and re-questioning of answers, which inevitably leads the traveler to a deeper and more profound knowledge and understanding of the subject being explored. The broadened perspective thus gained, is, in actuality, the acquisition of new cognitive tools, with which we are capable of mentally constructing our lodge.

The speculative nature of our Craft requires that we look beyond the conventional and apparent uses of the tools and symbols associated with our work, in order that we may truly gain knowledge, wisdom, and understanding (i.e., Light). It is for this purpose that this series of articles is being crafted. In this installment, we will explore the deep symbolism of the *Hour-Glass* as presented in Duncan's Masonic Monitor. The hourglass, also known as: a sand-glass, sand-timer, sand-clock, and egg timer, is a fascinating machine operationally used to measure time, and is dependent on the unseen forces of pressure and gravity acting on volume, mass and quantity. In addition to the use of the sand-based hourglass, Ancient Egyptians utilized a water-based time measuring machine known by its Latin name, clepsydra (water-clock). A preferred tool of seamen, the hourglass has been used to plot courses, measure distance, as well as track and monitor time.

The practicality and popularity of the hourglass is inherent in its simplicity. It uses very basic materials (sand, wood, glass) that are relatively easy to access and are easily calibrated in harmony with the sun while at its zenith. Its use as a symbol in Freemasonry is directly related to the journey of life, which mirrors the ancient Egyptian story of Ra (told in the Ancient Kemetic Lodge) where Ra represents the "Vital Essence" or the "Essence of Vitality." The ever-present (omnipresent) movement of cycles, symbolized by Khepra the dung beetle, is another ancient Egyptian symbol related to the hourglass in that it represents the self-perpetuating energies of life.

Duncan states:

The Hour-Glass

Is an emblem of human life. Behold! How swiftly the sands run, and how rapidly our lives are drawing to a close. We cannot without astonishment behold the little particles which are contained in this machine, how they pass away almost imperceptibly, and yet, to our surprise, in the short space of an hour they are all exhausted. Thus wastes man! To-

61

day he puts forth the tender leaves of hope; to-morrow blossoms, and bears his blushing honors thick upon him, the next day comes a frost, which nips the shoot, and, when he thinks his greatness still aspiring, he falls, like autumn leaves, to enrich old mother earth.

This lovely piece of prose gives a glimpse of the complexity of human life, and the uncertainty of the same, for those who are not raised to the sublime degree. For those Master Craftsmen among us, overstand that once the hourglass has run its course, we can simply invert (flip) the machine, setting time in motion, once again. The key is to exploit the very moment when the absolute last grain has attempted to exit the now vacant vessel and skillfully turn it as to never have a pause in the movement... thus is Life. Only those who do not have this "secret" understanding, perish and "waste" as Duncan has spoken.

Let's refer back to the substance of the hourglass, sand. Each individual grain of sand is symbolic of every precious moment experienced by all things Life. This is the profound notion encouraging all of life, as we know it, to live (animals, plants, minerals, spiritual, etc.). And just like each breath and passing moment contains a measure and degree of profundity, the grains of sand consist of a very complex, diverse, and highly stable molecule known as silicon dioxide (SiO_2). It has a tetrahedral or pyramidal structure (see figure 1) and is the most abundant mineral compound on the Earth's surface; just as Life. Silicon dioxide (also known as silica) is found in everything from sand to quartz crystals; similar to how DNA is found in all living things. In fact, silica is used to extract DNA from a cell's nucleus; making this an extraordinarily precise and highly functioning form of intelligence, just like life itself.

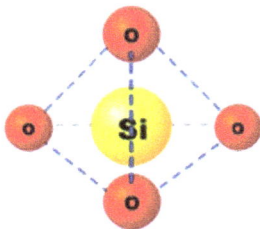

Figure 1. Model of a molecule of silicon dioxide (SiO_2).

The correlations between sand and life are infinite, each being just as profound as the next. Just as an opportunity resides in the passing of each individual grain, we are granted the opportunity to choose with the passing of each moment. Thus, by consciously choosing, every time there is a choice to be made, you are mentally taking your seat in the East, becoming the WM of your internal Lodge. In other words, intentionally making conscious decisions facilitates and increases the power of choice, thereby granting access to the true gift of exercising one's Will. And just as each grain is autonomous and has total integrity as an individual, the Brothers of the Lodge too function as a United-Independent body... which leads us into our topic for the next article, the Bee Hive.

The Bee Hive

Jeff Menzise, Ph.D., 32°, FPS

*F*ull of allegory and symbolism, our craft is one that both intrigues and strikes the uninitiated with awe. The strangeness of a language that does not readily lend itself to common interpretation is perhaps the most beneficial way of protecting sacred wisdom while simultaneously promoting the quest for "Light" outside of the Lodge. From the days of infancy, whether speaking of a newborn baby or a newly initiated E.A., the influx of new stimulation via the physical senses inspires the brain and mind to begin seeking answers. As a natural part of its process, this quest incorporates the questioning and re-questioning of answers, which inevitably leads the traveler to a deeper and more profound knowledge and understanding of the subject being explored. The broadened perspective thus gained, is, in actuality, the acquisition of new cognitive tools, with which we are capable of mentally constructing our "Grand Lodge," i.e., our body and mind.

Our Craft, being speculative in nature, requires us to look beyond the conventional and apparent uses of the tools and symbols associated with our work—if we are to truly gain Light. It is for this purpose that this series of articles is being crafted. In this second installment, we will explore the deep symbolism of the *Bee Hive* as presented in *Simon's Standard Masonic Monitor*. In order for us to comprehend the deep wisdom veiled by this extraordinary symbol, it would serve us well to first learn something of its maker...the bee.

Like its relatives, ants and wasps, bees live in colonies; tightly woven collectives of order, balance, reciprocity, justice and selflessness. In a bee colony, the work is never finished and the bee never tires nor strays from its task; and like all things in nature, bees are built for what they do. In the world of honeybees specifically, bees are built for one of three roles: the worker, the drone, or the queen. Worker bees are all female. They are perhaps the busiest bees in the hive carrying the responsibilities of: 1) building the hive, 2) guarding the hive, 3) nurturing the young, 4) scouting (for food sources and new potential locations for the hive), 5) foraging food and storing it, 6) distributing food to, and feeding the queen and her drones, 7) midwife to newly hatching drones, and, 8) getting rid of drones who have not mated. At some point in the course of their relatively short lives, each worker performs each of the above duties; typically rotating to a new station every three days (an interesting coincidence that these can correlate with eight positions in a masonic Lodge: WM, SW, SD, JW, JD, Secretary, Treasurer, and Tyler).

Each worker has special sacks in which they are able to store the nectar and pollen gathered on their daily missions. They have a gland in their abdomen that produces wax, with which they build their hives, and in their mouths and digestive tracts, exists an enzyme that begins to process the nectar into honey, also called the "golden nectar." This process takes place as foraging worker bees return to the hive and transfer their bounty to the household worker bees, eagerly awaiting their return and prized possession.

The drone bees are designed for one specific task, that is, to mate with the queen. These bees are all male and total only about 100 bees out of the 30,000 living in an average hive. These drones have larger bodies than the worker bees, no stinger and cannot store nectar and pollen. They have larger eyes designed to help them identify the queen when she is taking her "mating" flight. Like all things in nature, the drone does not outlive its purpose. Once the drone mates with the queen (in mid-flight) it dies by having its innards removed while still attached to her and is then carried back to the hive. Should a drone not mate and be found hanging around the hive, it is considered "dead weight" and is executed and removed from the hive by the worker bees.

Finally, the queen bee is a sort of slave to the hive. She is there for the sole purpose of reproducing and giving the colony a reason for existing; and is a central figure to serve and support. The reason for its existence, as defined by the queen, is the reproduction and continuation of the species. The queen is a peculiar creature because she begins as an "ordinary" egg, laid in a special region (Sanctum Sanctorum – Holy of Holies???) of the hive, where several other workers in the form of larvae, will be fed a special substance called "royal jelly," and thus, are transformed into queen bees, complete with the ability to lay almost 2 million eggs in their up to 4 years of life. When more than one queen is hatched, they must battle each other to the death. Typically the first queen to hatch has an advantage because she instinctively knows to sting the other queens before they completely emerge from their cells.

Interestingly, there are two situations in which the queen will leave a hive and take thousands of workers with her in search of a new location: 1) when there is a "draw" between two contending newly hatched queens, and 2) when the hive grows so large that it becomes crowded; it is then that the reigning queen departs with thousands of followers in search of a new place to build. Prior to the queen's departure, the remaining workers begin the process of creating another queen, which is unable to hatch until the original queen leaves. One other amazing fact about the queen bee is that she, by way of a chemical scent, renders the remaining females (workers) infertile, making them incapable of laying eggs.

As one can readily see by this discussion of the bee, there are many similarities between the bee and its hive, and the Freemason and his Lodge. According to Simon's Standard Masonic Monitor, the bee hive:

> ...is an emblem of industry, and recommends the practice of that virtue to all created beings, from the highest seraph in heaven to the lowest reptile of the dust. It teaches us that as we came into the world rational and intelligent beings, so we should ever be industrious ones; never sitting down contented while our fellow-creatures around us are in want, especially when it is in our power to relieve them without inconvenience to ourselves.

When we take a survey of Nature, we

view man in his infancy, more helpless and indigent than the brute creation; he lies languishing for days, months and years, totally incapable of providing sustenance for himself, of guarding against the attack of the wild beasts of the field, or sheltering himself from the inclemencies of the weather. It might have pleased the great Creator of heaven and earth to have mankind independent of all created beings; but as dependence is one of the strongest bonds of society, mankind were made dependent on each other for protection and security, thereby enjoying better opportunities of fulfilling the duties of reciprocal love and friendship. Thus was man formed for social and active life, the noblest part of the work of God; and he who will so demean himself as not to endeavor to add to the common stock of knowledge may be deemed a drone in the hive of nature, a useless member of society, and unworthy of our protection as Masons.

Just as our Craft is divided into three degrees (E.A., F.C., M.M.), so, too, is the bee's body separated into three: the thorax, the abdomen, and the head (see Image 1). Each section corresponds perfectly to one another in the following ways: The abdomen aligns with the work of the E.A. in that it is the physical and often unenlightened aspect of human beingness. The candidate at this stage is still in darkness seeking Light, and depends on its God-given instincts and

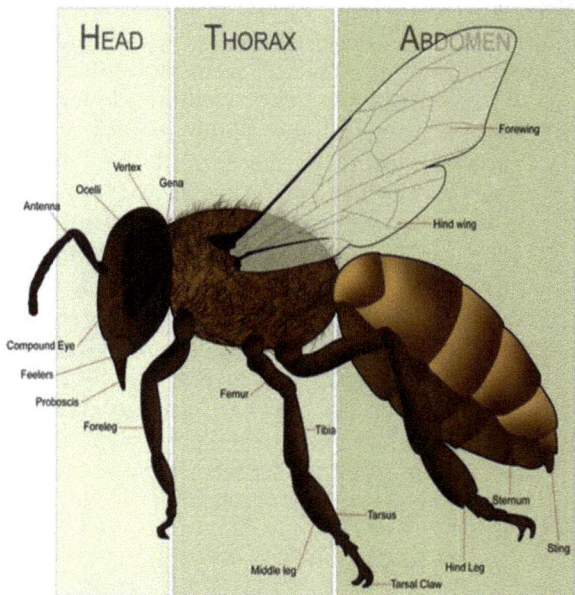

Image 1. The anatomy of the bee is divided into three sections, each specializing in a particular function for the bee and its hive.
Image credit: https://www.buzzaboutbees.net/honey-bee-anatomy.html

physical nature to understand and solve its problems. The abdomen of a bee contains the bee's digestive organs and major defense apparatus, the stinger with its venom. It is from this end of the creature that a sacrifice of its own life is made, in defense of the hive (bees die after stinging because their internal organs remain attached to the stinger as they pull away from the threat, which literally disembowels them). Not knowing any other option, the E.A. similarly places his own life on the Altar as a symbol of devotion and commitment to his fellow travelers.

The thorax of the worker bee lines up perfectly with the F.C., because it is during this time that the candidate begins to learn and work in materials. They are sent out to the quarry, only to return with the resources necessary for building the temple. In the world of bees, the materials are both harvested and created by internal processes; thus the bees literally give of their own substance in order to create their hives. In other words, it is within the abdomen that bees generate the wax from which their hexagonical cells are formed (see

Image 2), however, it is from the thorax that they actually manipulate the materials with their legs, and travel using wings to fly.

The wax may be paper-thin in some places and a hive as light as a feather, yet it can hold and maintain pounds of honey. This amazing fact and feat is attributed to the design and layout of the hive. It is the precise shape of the six-sided cells that allow for the maximum use of space and provides the perfect and only environment for hatching new bees. The F.C., like the worker bee, is totally devoted to its work

Image 2. The hexagon shape of each cell is specially designed to maximize space and to guarantee the growth of new bees.

and its Lodge, and is learning to use his tools and materials for the benefit of the whole organization, under the command of the W.M. and other M.M. in the Lodge.

The head of the worker bee aligns with the M.M. degree within the lodge in that it is the thinking and reasoning aspect of the bee. It is here that the bee receives its impulse to build in the patterns instinctively given to it; it is from here that bees communicate the tasks and needs of the hive to one another; it is from this high point that the bee is capable of functioning according to plan. Those who have mastered the study of bees have identified an aspect of bee life that is only found in humans and other lower primates: the ability to communicate through symbolic means. This gift is specifically found in what has been termed the "waggle dance." This "dance" is performed by a scouting and foraging worker-bee who has found a viable source of food. The bee upon its return, begins to communicate the location of resources by symbolic gestures and sounds, certain signs and movements, a song and dance. The other workers, who are being recruited for the task of mining this newly found resource, gather around and are seen observing and learning the new information. One other amazing aspect of this dance is that the instructions are based on the location of the sun (Light). Any clear-minded M.M. has already seen the parallel between this process and the T.B., upon which the W.M. and G.A.O.T.U. draws plans in symbolic fashion, in hopes of leading their lodge towards the Light, our most coveted resource.

One other very important correlation between the work of bees and the M.M. is found in the fact that while the bees are busying themselves seeking pollen and nectar, they are simultaneously serving all of creation. They assist in the spreading of pollen from one bloom to the next, without which, vegetative reproduction would cease. They simultaneously provide so much of the sweetness that we humans, and many other creatures, enjoy in the form of healing honeys, pollens, royal jelly, and wax. This is directly reflected by the true M.M. who also serves all of humanity in his quest for more Light, through the principle of Charity. He, by virtue of living his oaths, becomes a beacon of light for others who may be engulfed by darkness, not realizing they even need Light. This is done without a single thought beyond their self-proclaimed, willfully accepted, and self-imposed task of going from good to better.

The hive itself is an amazing piece of architecture and follows a plan that is un-seen by the profane, and is only evidenced by the existence of hives built according to the same principles. Much like our T.B., the plans are coded symbolically, and carry within them the key to a fruitful and pro-ductive life. In order to build a structure such as the bee hive, bees must be master builders; fully capable of taking the raw materials (rough ashlar), processing them into a state fit for use in the construction of their hive (perfect ashlar). The bees must value their hive for what it is: the protec-tor of their way of life, the keeper of their secrets, and the place wherein they are able to guarantee their future generations are able to carry on tradition. This is exemplified by the presence of worker bees who serve as guardians to the opening of their hives.

Bees literally have Tylers at the entrance of the hive.

These Tylers are there to prevent "Cowans," in the form of rodents and insects, from entering the hive. Similar to our Order, there are sometimes individuals who are capable of giving the proper signs and due-guards necessary for gaining entrance; in the world of bees, one of the greatest infiltrators is known as the *Death's Head Hawk Moth* (see Image 3). This brilliant insect is capable of imitating the chemical signature of the bee (its sign and due-guard), producing a smell that is consistent with

Image 3. The *Death's Head Hawk Moth* is an interesting insect fully capable of entering into the beehive. Notice the symbolic "skull" on its back as well as the pattern similar to a bee's.

others in the hive. This allows for the moth to gain entrance into the hive and partake of the life sustaining honey stored therein. Similar to our Lodges, the bees are not overly suspicious of the "stranger" amongst them, having full trust in their Tyler to screen and divert any potential impostor. And just like our Lodges, eavesdroppers and Cowans are sometimes able to temporarily gain entrance, although this is a very dangerous form of treachery.

One other interesting fact, relating to the securing of the hive, is that each hive is kept totally antibacterial, antiviral, and, antifungal by virtue of the materials and forms used in its building. A bee hive is one of the cleanest places on earth. (Image 4.)

The bee, as a symbol, can be traced far back into antiquity. It is a noble image used to represent various concepts. In ancient Egypt (Kemet), the bee was used to symbolize the sovereignty of the King, establishing their will as being second only to that of God. This symbolism was carried by the "Red Crown," which also demonstrated the martial aspect of self-defense,

Image 4. The beehive is a magnificent structure whose form is based purely on its function and according to an encoded and symbolic plan.

which is sometimes necessary to defend one's personal and collective rights. This use correlates strongly with the Masonic notion that each man is a sovereign, free to govern himself according to his degree of knowledge and wisdom; two characteristics that can be trained and cultivated in all men who earnestly seek enlightenment.

The Merovingians (a Salin Frankish dynasty ruling in what was known as Gaul in the 5th century) used the bee to symbolize immortality and resurrection. This use corresponds directly with the story of H.A., and is demonstrated by the drone bee who dies during the act of mating, only to be resurrected in the fertilized eggs being laid by the queen. Another relationship between the Merovingians' use of the bee and immortality is found in the life giving and generative properties found in the bee's royal jelly, pollen, and honey. In the Islamic V of S.L., the Holy Quran, there is an entire chapter devoted to the bee, Sura 16 Al-Nahl. In verses 68 and 69, it is written of the industrious and sovereign nature of bees and how they produce an elixir of life for all to partake in.

In closing, the symbolism of the bee is quite profound and is the example par excellence of what being a Master builder is all about. The M.M. who studies and reflects upon the bee and its lodge (hive), and who earnestly seeks to apply this wisdom to his own life (through the law of analogy), will find his craft and quest for light enhanced. Just as the ancients looked to nature to better understand those natural aspects of themselves, we as Craftsmen would benefit to do the same. So the next time you see a bee, resist the urge to swat at it. Calm the sense of fear, which has been programmed from childhood as a defense against getting stung; instead, observe it in a humble and thankful manner for we have been provided with a living symbol, from which to learn and model.

The Evolving Masonic Mind

Jeff Menzise, Ph.D., 32°, FPS

"Thus some that were once creeping things change into things that in the water dwell, the Souls of water things change to earth dwellers, those that live on the earth change into things with wings, and Souls that live in the air change into men, while the human Souls reach the first steps of Deathlessness."

– Corpus Hermeticum, The Key

*T*he above quote from the *Corpus Hermeticum* provides a straight-forward perspective on the notion of evolution. It weds the concepts of physical and meta-physical evolution, alluding to the more noble notion of "the evolution of Consciousness." There is, however, a step missing from this otherwise perfect analogy, in that it begins with "creeping things" that become water dwellers. You will see that three of the four elements (Water, Earth, Air) are mentioned with an almost intentional neglect of the fourth, Fire. If you observe the progression laid out by the analogy, you will see that creatures have gone from the interior of our planet, out towards the atmosphere, eventually returning internal by-way of approaching a "Deathless" state as the human Soul.

Following this line of thinking, and by stepping back a bit to get a broader view of the subject, we can easily see that the original phase of creation/consciousness would've existed at the core of the planet, which is literally a ball of Fire so intense that it contains every element that exists on any other level of this planet (submerged by Water, upon the Earth, or within the Air) in it's rawest and most simplified form.

These elements rise through gaseous vents, liquid streams of magma, or as solid particles in order to create, mix, and mingle with the forms found in the water above. They continue to rise through the

Water, some being consumed by the life forms dwelling on the ocean's floor (a dense version of the liquified and gaseous core) which then are consumed by those that patrol the border separating the deepest parts of the ocean from those above, and so forth until they reach the upper regions that mix with air and earth. Here they are further consumed by the "things with wings," humans, and "creeping things." Archaeologists and geologist have long confirmed that decaying prehistoric life now exist as oil and other minerals found deep within the earth, from which they are recycled back into the process.

It seems that the most intriguing parts of this perpetual cycle, as outlined by the opening quote, are the Alpha and Omega, the beginning and the end; specifically, the point of origins and the final destination. In the beginning the GAOTU said "Let there be Light..." We all know there can be no light without the warmth of fire. We also know, and agree, that the Soul of Man (Sol-O-Mon – Sol meaning Sun) is Immortal, and that the purpose of our Ancient Mysteries is to assist Man to consciously realize this, prior to experiencing the "death" of his physical body. In this one quote, we have the blueprint for the Ancient process designed to make "Good Men Better," and to raise them from the dead, to a living p_____r.

To some, it may seem that I am reaching by making such a bold and profound statement about this one line of "prose." Such an assertion is totally understandable, and betrays the degree of development of the one making such a claim. You cannot expect, or at least you should not expect, a child to understand things and grasp concepts that are beyond their degree of development. Will Smith in the first "Men In Black" movie demonstrated this while being tested for his worthiness of joining the elite organization. Recall the scene where he and several other high-ranking military officials were at the shooting range. They were tasked with taking out "the enemy." Everyone except Will Smith's character began to shoot the images of aliens that were interspersed throughout the course.

Will Smith took one single shot, penetrating the forehead of a young, blond-haired girl carrying a stack of books. When questioned about his choice, he pointed out how each of the aliens in the scene were doing things as simple as exercising and blowing their nose, but the little girl posed a threat because she was carrying a quantum physics book. She obviously was not who and what she portrayed herself to be. In this regard, he was serving as a Tyler, exposing and penalizing an imposter, a "cowan" of sorts. Not only did Will Smith outperform the other candidates who were all highly-skilled, but he did so by demonstrating a certain degree of consciousness that was all but vacant in the other prospects, regardless of their rankings within their respective organizations. Throughout the examination, Will Smith's character solved problems via intuition and various adaptations; all of which demonstrated a particular and unique insight and ability.

To close this example, I will point out one last, very interesting observation. When Will Smith was offered a position with the "Men in Black" agency (who just happen to be wearing black suits and black ties), he took some time to reflect on the weight of such a position. He sat on the banks of a river watching the sunset. He sat there until the sun rose over the horizon, emerging with a sense of clarity that can only be provided by the reception of Light, after coming out of darkness. This simultaneously alludes to the Ancient initiation text of East African origins loosely called "The Book of Coming Forth By Day," or "The Book of Coming Into the Light," called by the Egyptians themselves, "Per-t Em Heru," which has incorrectly been called by its more popular name "The Book of the Dead."

Brother Menzise, why begin a dissertation on The Evolving Masonic Mind with such a discussion? I am glad you asked. The purpose is to provide an analogy by which we may witness the advancement, even if fictional, of consciousness that must exist aware only of the things related to its current and sometimes earlier levels. A human analogy, from the perspective of Piaget's theory of cognitive development, specifically his notion of "object permanence," will serve our understanding well. Piaget illustrated how very young children experience the notion of "out of sight, out of mind."

They literally believe that to not see is for it to not be. This is why a child playing "hide and go seek," or who wishes to simply disappear, will cover and/or close their eyes; believing that because they can't see you, you can't see them.

As adults, because we have all gone through that particular stage of cognitive development long ago, it is difficult for us to fathom how such a line of reasoning is possible. However, on a subconscious level, we still play out this understanding by closing our eyes when we wish to not be seen or to "disappear" in a fear-induced state. The success of camera-based security systems, and the tactics used by law enforcement designed to catch drivers speeding down the highway, rests on this earlier phase of cognition that remains active on the unconscious levels of human thinking. When a thief can't see the camera recording their actions, they feel they are not being viewed, and therefore carry on with their actions.

This also plays itself out on the internet which provides a certain degree of distance, invisibility, and anonymity for users who are less confident in expressing their views to others they can literally see and touch (or who can see and touch them); a fact that many have theorized to lead to the aggressive and hypersexual environment found within the tangles of the world wide web.

Let us now return to our earlier analogy inspired by the opening quote. The life forms found at the core of the earth, although undiscovered at this point (but which more likely than not exist based on the fact that life is present on ALL other layers of this planet), are aware of the things on their level. Those that dwell on the ocean floor experience life only as it exists on the ocean floor: in almost absolute darkness, therefore functioning without photosynthesis (and other processes vital and necessary for life on "higher" levels), and are fully capable of withstanding extreme atmospheric pressure that would immediately crush any life form attempting to dive deeper than their capacity to withstand. Also of importance, is the fact that life on the ocean floor is based upon the foundation laid by life at the core of the earth. This is demonstrated by the life-giving and sustaining minerals that spew from the vents found on the ocean floor, which are then ingested by the various life-forms dwelling there. This is a concrete example of the interdependency of each level; one upon another.

Let's take a little more time to further illustrate these degrees of interdependency by highlighting the life of several species of whale. These amazing mammals are some of the largest known creatures in the world, and can be found dwelling in almost every layer above the deepest depths of the ocean, and yet, are required to rise to the surface in order to breath the air above. They span one of the most diverse of all known ecological systems, carrying traits that, according to our surface and human reasoning, defy all logic. One clear example is the Sperm Whale, its astonishing size, and ability to devour tons of giant squid. Some Sperm Whales produce feces that is valued more than gold in some markets. This is because of its unique properties (including smell) and use by certain high-end perfume companies such as Chanel, for their signature scent Chanel No. 5.

The Humpback Whale, like all baleen (toothless) whales, also travels between the various layers of the ocean, and is unique because, despite its size, it survives mostly on krill and other small sea creatures. The Blue Whale also survives mostly on krill, and it is considered the largest living mammal on the planet. The Cuvier's Beaked Whale carries the record for the deepest dive, registering at over 6,000 feet. Each of the whales mentioned above, specifically those without teeth, survive on diets consisting largely of phytoplankton. Looking closely at the name of this microscopic creature, we will find the word "phyto" which is Greek for "plant." This indicates that these microscopic creatures have chlorophyll, and therefore, are designed to capture sunlight and process it for nutrients and energy, which they subsequently pass on to the whales that consume them. Another interesting fact is that these tiny organisms are known to rival the oxygen production of massive forests found on the earth's surface. For one of our planet's largest creatures to survive almost solely on one of our planet's smallest life forms is paradoxical, but a perfect example of how all of creation is always interdependent, in all ways.

The human body consists of various closed systems, each having a clear line of delineation, separating one from another. Brilliantly, each system also has clear marks of interdependency and interconnectedness with every other system. Our Ancient Ancestors took this knowledge and based their philosophical and scientific practices upon it. For example, they correlated each organ system with the four (sometimes five)elements as they are found operating in nature; drawing direct relationships to the physical, mental, and spiritual aspects of human-beingness. Both Ancient African as well as Ancient Asian scientists classified the organ systems, diseases, and symptoms, according to the "Five Elements." These Elements are: Air, Earth, Fire, Water, Metal (sometimes Wood).

The digestive system, for example, is said to contain both the Fire and Water elements, engaging one another by way of digestion (Fire) and the distribution and assimilation of resources (Water). The respiratory system embodies the elements of Fire, Water, and Air. Air is easy to recognize because it is literally what is being inhaled and exhaled; the presence of Fire and Water are a bit more cryptic. At one level, Fire is present in the oxygen itself, which is required for any fire to burn. Within our bodies, it is the oxygen alongside glucose that provides the fuel used in the process of aerobic cellular respiration. Interestingly, Water (literal H_2O) is a by-product of this process. Fire is also present by way of the relationship between the circulatory system and the respiratory system (Cardiopulmonary system). The circulatory system, as controlled and conducted by the Heart as its Master, is used to transport both the waste and nutritive products brought in by the digestive system, as well as the respiratory system, which is a function of Water.

In a healthy system, the heartbeat, and therefore the heart rate, can be controlled and regulated by the rate of breathing maintained by the organism. If one breathes faster, the heart will follow suit and begin to beat faster. There are ways to individuate these rates, an exercise that has life sustaining and protective results, often enjoyed by those who are trained in the practical applications of meditation and other forms of energy manipulation.

For the majority of us, this relationship is often overlooked and left to be manipulated by our emotions and environmental triggers of whose existence, to a great degree, we remain unaware. To further illustrate this relationship, I often use the analogy of the bellow and the fire. As stated above, fire depends on oxygen for its existence. This is why we use a bellow to sustain an existing fire in our fireplaces, or gently blow on a glowing ember in hopes of our breath inspiring the fire to grow.

The bellows and the action of opening and closing, imitates the inhaling and exhaling of the lungs, the inspiration and expiration of oxygen, and the corresponding heart rate (beating of the heart), reflects the strength of the fire. Think about a raging, but quickly diminished fire. This is akin to the sudden increase in breathing and heart rate experienced by a person who has

95

been scared by a predator in their environment, and therefore motivated into evasive action.

The spike is immediately and intensely felt, but quickly gives way to a sense of overall depletion. This is like the fire I mentioned in my book Symbolically Speaking vol. 1, that manifests in the forms of a bonfire created using gasoline, or by an intense, but short-lived bolt of lightning. Contrastingly, the trained long-distance runner utilizes very specific rates and techniques of breathing, in order to generate a sustained quality of energy, used to carry their physical and mental bodies over great distances; this is analogous to the sustained and regulated shining of our Sun.

This opening dialogue is designed to awaken the plasticity of our thinking minds, in hopes of producing a certain level of receptivity I feel is necessary to gain maximum benefit from the discussion that is to follow. The above use of analogy, and the requisite mental gymnastics, will hopefully serve as the mallet used to tenderize meat prior to the sprinkling on of seasonings that will bring our final product to an exquisite end result; rendering us fully capable of internalizing the insights to be shared regarding the "evolving Masonic mind." Without said preparations, we may very well end up with a bland taste in our mouths regarding the otherwise nutritious substance we are set to devour. Having laid the ground work for our forthcoming labor, I would like to now guide us into the deeper discussion of our topic, directing us to look further into our "Degree Work."

It is my expressed position that our Masonic degrees and ritual are designed to inspire and motivate the evolution of our capabilities as humans, with each degree ushering in the cognitive and spiritual advancement according to its type. As Brothers, being divested of our material goods and waiting in the antechamber of the Lodge, we carry one degree of consciousness. This degree is dominated by a desire for "more Light." This desire presupposes an acknowledgement of varying degrees of Light, the possession of a certain amount of Light, and the possibility of their being Light beyond what one is currently experiencing.

Before making the conscious decision to enter upon this journey, many of us were totally unaware of the "all encompassing Light," in which we are constantly bathed, and constantly ingesting (physiologically and literally via the melanin in our skin, hair, and eyes; by way of the foods we ingest that got it via the chlorophyll of plants; cognitively by our learning faculties; emotionally by the interactions we have with other living beings in our environment, etc.). Going from that antechamber to the awaiting Altar within, we are slowly but surely made more and more aware of this Light, it's various degrees of intensity, and how those individual rays shape the reality around us.

Each and every degree, as stated, should make us more and more aware of the existing Light. Meaning a person existing as an E.A., should have less conscious control over, and awareness of Light, than a person standing on the Square of a M.M. The way we delineate one degree of Light from another purely exists on the cognitive level, specifically by what information one has obtained: the specific gr____p, s___gn

and d_____d associated with a particular degree; all of which is memorized but
not necessarily understood. Unfortunately,
it is not required for Brothers to develop an
understanding of the symbolism and processes contained within the degree work,
in order to advance to the next degree. This
becomes problematic because, based on
Ancient expressions of our modern practices, our degree work is literally supposed to
open us to an elevated means by which to
engage, master, and manipulate what we
understand to be reality. This means that
a Master Mason should be fully capable of
engaging in a discussion about an everyday
object, in a way that differs, in both quality
and form, from that of an E.A. or a non-Mason. Again, I am not merely referring to our
abilities to use certain jargon and intellec-
tual references, but speak specifically of a
demonstrated understanding of the subject
on ever-deepening levels and degrees.

For example, I would consider a
non-Masonic discussion of an apple to be
argumentative and centered around whether or not an apple is actually an apple. This
type of discourse betrays the inability of an

individual's mind to conceive of, and process, an apparent reality. This can be due to physical blindness, or mental stubbornness. The former is understandable and excusable, the latter, not so much. We have all experienced situations in which either we, ourselves, or someone with whom we are engaged in a conversation, has been stubborn to the point of denying a verifiable truth that exists right before their eyes.

We perhaps experience this everyday when someone seems to argue simply for the sake of arguing, refusing to accept the fact that maybe, just maybe, there is insight and information beyond what they have been exposed to, or received. We are all incorrect at one point or another, even the most "evolved" of us. This level of arguing is more about the attitude of the one doing the arguing. It is often coming from a place of rigidity and purposeful ignorance, meaning they know they don't know, but pretend as if they do for the sake of maintaining a position they have always purported, or simply to "save face."

A slightly more advanced perspective, that of an E.A., acknowledges the apple, but wants to debate on the type of apple. Initiating a debate on this a level does not require any true depth, but instead centers on the fact that the apple is either red, green, or yellow in color. The discussion remains very concrete and factual. The limitations of this sort of discussion rests in the fact that too much time and energy are utilized debating relatively trivial matters.

This level often expends vast amounts of energy attempting to formulate arguments that sound the best, and are more creative in their way of expressing the simplest of notions. This degree of Light is useful because it provides the building blocks of analytical thinking (breaking the whole down into parts), which is required by anyone interested in developing the synthetical skill of part-whole thinking, i.e., being able to see that the forest is made up of individual trees, and understanding what that means for the whole forest. Lots of our historically-driven research falls into this category. This is where we find the notion that "it cannot be unless we have found documented evidence to prove that it is." It relates back to our earlier discussion on "object permanence," and the concept of "out of sight, out of mind." One of my favorite quotes from The Boondocks animated television series is, "The absence of evidence is not the evidence of absence." I like to give credit to the cartoon; however, the cartoon actually quotes astronomer Carl Sagan.

This level of argument, for example, is used to say there is no life on other planets. In recent years, while pondering such a notion, I began to question our current definitions of life, which are totally based on our limited, earth-bound experiences of life. Meaning, we are using earth-based tools and techniques to determine if there is life existing on Mars, or elsewhere in this vast and perhaps infinite universe. This perspective is limited because, to us, "life" is carbon-based, and manifests very specific traits like reproduction, consumption, etc. When searching for life on other planets and in other environments, we typically use these traits as our standard. If we don't see these things, we conclude that no life present.

Our explorations must start some-
where, and a good definition is an excellent
launchpad. What's even more important is
the flexibility of mind to know that where
we are starting is itself limited by our current knowledge and perspective. To think
that we have it all figured out, simply because we can count and measure & develop
awesome technologies, is to arrogantly run
in an ever-widening circle, believing that we
are actually advancing on a linear trajectory
of growth and understanding.

Let's go to deep space for our next
example of the limitations of this degree
of thinking, perceiving, reasoning, and
knowing. The modern and Western understanding of the Sirius star system is in its
infancy, as compared to the understanding
displayed by the Dogon of Mali, West Africa.
The Dogon have demonstrated a deep
knowledge of this distant binary star system
(Sirius A & Sirius B) as recorded in their alle-
gories, rituals, and daily practically-applied
knowledge. They had no telescopes as we
know, but clearly have been able to chart
the movement of these stars. Prior to the
late 1800s, Western astronomers had no

clue of the existence of Sirius B, and there-fore, had no idea why the Dogon said and did what that do in certain ritual aspects of their culture.

The Western understanding is still very limited, even with the "discovery" of the correlations between the Sirius solar system and the Dogon society. Some claim that a French explorer must have told the Dogon of the star system, leading to their ritual ceremony of circumambulating in a pattern that copies that of Sirius B orbiting Sirius A. And what must also explain how they knew of the magnificent density of Sirius B, referring to it as the "Po Star," after a small but potent grain they use. As a side note, Sirius B is not visible to the naked eye due in part to its own declining lumi-nescence, but also because Sirius A shines so much brighter. This made it impossible for Westerners to calculate its density until recently, specifically in 2005.

This demonstrates how looking di-rectly into the brightest of lights, can actu-ally blind you to what is hidden right before your eyes. This is a magnificent clue as to how we are to advance beyond this degree, fully embracing the growth that comes with understanding. This notion also gives a clue to what is perhaps a subtle purpose of the h_____k. Is it possible that by restricting the use of our eyes, we are forced to utilize other senses in our quest for knowledge? Could this staple in our Masonic quest actually be designed to shut down the organ typically used to detect and process Light, in order to awaken other ways of Knowing?

Notice how visually impaired people, specifically those who are legally blind, tend to have a heightened sense of awareness that depends partially on their other senses, but also greatly on their intuitive abilities. In my own African initiations, I have experienced the restriction of the visual apparatus for extended periods of time, during which I was encouraged, if not forced, to awaken new faculties that go well beyond the detection and perception of what is physically measurable; an experience that has afforded me a degree of insight and knowledge not commonly found amongst non-initiates. Our Masonic Craft once carried this same opportunity and task. What will it take to reclaim it?

This degree of reasoning also causes some, in knee-jerk fashion, to declare that Freemasonry did not exist in Ancient Kemet (Egypt), simply because they do not find the word, or its "equivalent" in the Kemetic (Egyptian) writings. A great deal of these detractors do not comprehend the Ancient Egyptian culture, spirituality, worldview, nor their writings, but are adamant about what it did not contain. This opposition is contrary to all of the physical evidence that exists within what remains of Ancient Egypt in the form of columns, buildings in stone, their advanced understanding of human nature, and many other indicators.

This reminds me of a discussion I once had with an astrologer who tried hard to convince me that Aquarius was actually an "Air" sign, as listed in popular, modern astrology. My position is that it is a water sign; a position that is much easier to defend than the notion that it is an "Air" sign. For example, the symbol for Aquarius is the "Water-bearer," and in the word itself, you find the word "aqua" which literally means water. Now of course there is moisture in some air, which makes some air a water bearer, however, it takes a greater leap to relate Aquarius to Air, than it does to equate it with water.

A similar argument is launched against the notion that Ancient Egyptians had one of the earliest practices of Yoga, a science of the mind-body-spirit that is often thought to be of Indian origins. Of course you don't see the word Yoga in Egyptian literature, or any other Sanskrit words describing these practices. What you do have, hidden in plain sight, are yoga postures carved into stone, all throughout the Nile Valley. If one knows the meaning of the word "Yoga," then they can recognize that the Egyptian phrase "Smai Tawi," has a similar meaning of "linking or joining an upper and lower aspect of the same entity." In our Masonic Craft, we find a similar meaning in the "Star of David," also known as the "Seal of Solomon." The triangle pointing upwards symbolizes our spiritual and higher nature, while the triangle pointing downwards, our physical and base nature. If you superimpose this symbol onto the compasses and square, you find an almost exact alignment both in meaning, and in form.

The ability to see and comprehend these correlations is a function of developing higher aspects of our human abilities. These aspects typically go beyond the concrete-based knowledge and understanding that are currently held as the pinnacle of human abilities. It's this type of thinking, and value system, that allows for scientists to conduct dangerous experiments to "block-out" certain rays of the sun, in an attempt to address "global warming." To embark upon such an endeavor demonstrates what happens when non-initiates are given the power to do as they wish. There is a movie called ***Snowpiercer*** that shows precisely how this sort of experiment ends.

Passing on to the next step, we shall look into what a F.C. degree of Light brings to the discussion of an apple. A F.C. has accepted the fact that the apple exists, and has discerned the existing type of apple based on its color and particular breed of apple. The next step is to be able to take that knowledge and information, and develop a sophisticated degree of understanding (collectively called "Light"). This form of thinking is a bit more efficient than the previous degrees because it is not expending time nor resources on debating the trivial and easily verifiable aspects of the subject; instead, this degree focuses more on what these variations mean, and perhaps, how they derived.

This degree acknowledges the vibratory difference between the Red Delicious, the Golden Delicious, and the Granny Smith. This vibratory difference manifests as a difference in color, smell, taste, and subsequent reaction of the salivary glands of the mouth, and the varying nutritional substance provided by the digestive process. In other words, this degree of consciousness seeks to apply the Light to develop a deeper understanding of purpose, and how purpose determines, and perhaps dictates, both the form and function of a thing. Light at this level is required for us to benefit from analogy, allegory, and symbolism. Hence, the reason we are considered Craftsmen at our 2nd Degree.

As Craftsmen, we are entrusted with the ability and responsibility of carrying the tools of a M.M., even those for which we are not yet qualified to use, but that are required by the M.M. with whom we are training. This is symbolized by the way we wear our a___n at this stage. Carrying these tools, even without the requisite knowledge of how to use them, demonstrates our receptivity and desire to learn more about what we possess, and that we are being prepared for a greater responsibility.

This phenomenal degree of understanding, as great as it is, is still limited by the boundaries of the degree-work, and the resulting limited consciousness thereby awakened. This limited consciousness tends to remain physically-based, meaning it is still just a deeper dive into the physically-tangible aspects of the subject; in this case the apple. It can get as sophisticated as the knowledge a master chemist yields about an apple; complete with a discourse on the chemical composition of the various skin colors, sugar content, caloric count, rate of decomposition, etc. As valuable as this perspective is, there are still deeper and brighter degrees of Light to be shined.

Here, we find ourselves seeking that which lies beyond the veil of physical reality. As we dive deeper into the chemical contents of our proverbial apple, we begin to realize that what we see on the outside, is totally dependent on these microscopic and therefore unseen bits of energy, matter, and natural forces. We begin to understand that the physical structures we have come to depend so heavily upon, are illusory at their core. We begin to appreciate the notion that the majority of "creation" consists of space between small bits of matter, and that we exist in a microcosmic form of the greater universe, and as a macrocosmic form of the microworlds we are beginning to explore.

The Marvel Universe movies, *Ant-man* and *Doctor Strange*, explore these subatomic and non-physical worlds in a manner that is both entertaining and informed. Many non-Western societies have demonstrated knowledge of these various worlds that exist beyond our ability to physically sense and perceive. The earlier Dogon example is one, the many findings and understandings of the Ancient Egyptians is another, and also the many deep wisdom traditions found amongst those living in the South and Central American jungles, bear witness to this truth.

In each of these civilizations, you find a systematic process, commonly referred to as a Rites of Passage, designed to heighten, awaken, and refine, the innate abilities of Man. You immediately see the difference between those within a society that have been initiated as compared to those who have not been; and can even see the difference between how these societies fared when their cultures and initiation systems were fully intact; as compared to when they were forcibly removed by invading colonizers. I often liken our current situation as descendants of the African Lodge Masons (PHA), to the plight of civilizations that have lost their original culture and way of life. We would likely be much further ahead of our current situation: financially, spiritually, academically, socially, and definitely in our overall well-being.

In order to maximize our experiences at this level of development, we must become proficient at seeing and truly understanding the "speculative" use of our working tools. It is not enough to be able to recite what is being proclaimed by our ritual. We must take that next step to actually seek an understanding of how the Trowel, for example, is used "to spread the cement of Brotherly love." To comprehend this, we will need to simultaneously see both the literal aspect of spreading cement, as well as the figurative suggestion of the existence of a different kind of cement used to bond Men, one to another. This further implies the necessity of some sort of preparation and internal work.

Similar to building with stone and brick, we must make sure that we have the proper "cement" and that the materials to be bonded have be primed for this purpose. In some cases, the sides to be bonded must be made rough through the use of a high-grade sandpaper, in other cases, we may need the sides to be as smooth as possible.

Either way, the materials, in this case people, must be duly prepared by removing all that would prevent the bonding, and by strengthening those attributes designed to facilitate the process.

On the M.M. degree, the Light should raised from physical properties to a more philosophical and less tangible expression. Light at this degree makes the leap from the creeping to water, from water to earth, from earth to air, and from air to human, and onto the Immortal stage (interestingly "The Immortals" is how the 3rd degree is identified in both George G.M. James' account of the first three degrees of the Egyptian Mysteries, and in Dr. T.M. Stewart's account). This line of evolution as presented at the opening of this discourse, gives the allusion of leaving behind the merely physical comprehension of a subject in order to embrace its more subtle and non-tangible aspects; specifically, those aspects that go beyond feeding bodies, but are instead, designed to nourish the mind and eventually our Souls.

A person on this level of reasoning

has accepted and internalized the understandings presented and taught at previous
stages. Those degrees serve as the step-
ping-stones to realizing that the physical
and tangible "nature" of all things, is based
upon their invisible and non-tangible aspects. This was symbolized by the Ancient
Egyptian principle called "Amen," and made
active by Ptah at the potter's wheel, and
Khepera, the dung beetle, as the notion of
perpetual creation—generating all-things
from no-thing.

Sticking with our apple analogy, the
question has advanced far beyond the initial
debate of whether this is an apple, and even
well beyond the question of the type of
apple, its purpose, and subsequent impact
on other physical realities. At this degree of
enLightenMent, the Master Mason realizes
he can "count the number of seeds in an
apple, but has no clue the number of apples
in a seed." This notion projects the vast and
innumerable benefits that have yet to be
derived by embracing the infinite nature of
Light. It is from this platform that the M.M.
should "seek more Light outside of the
Lodge."

The individual who has truly awakened their capacity to receive and engage this degree of Light is, as Stewart notes, "living his life in accord with his ideals of equity, justice and right, [and therefore] his spiritual powers began to unfold. He became aware of his own transformation; the proof of which was gradually revealed to him in the widening of his power of apprehension; the deepening of his power for comprehension; and the growth of the faculty of intuition." Stewart continues by quoting Philo's perspective and understanding of the Egyptian Initiate: "This race, my son, is never taught, but when he willeth it, its memory is restored by God...For there is, my son, a Word of Wisdom that no tongue can tell, a Holy Word about the Lord of All, the God before all thought, whom to declare transcends all human power."

With this mental and cognitive exercise behind us, I would now like to turn our Light onto the final subject of our current dissertation: US currency in the form of the two dollar bill. It is my primary goal, through the writing of the following lecture, to present the reader with a more in-depth and enlightened discussion of a symbol that has brought a significant amount of debate to our Craft. I would like for us to take the perspective of Masters, as described above, recognizing that there are levels on which we can engage in this conversation that go: beyond the debates that take place in the antechamber; that go as deep as the cavern in which my Companion's and I found the missing Keystone; and onto even deeper levels of comprehension guarded by our Shriners, Sublime Princes, Sovereign Grand Inspector Generals, and the Knights Templars among us.

It is my prayer that the tough nature of our minds has been relaxed and rendered receptive to a line of thinking, supported by facts and research, that goes beyond our common dependencies on what we consider to be worthy of consideration, reaching well into those deepest regions of mind, where, like the depths of the ocean, "common" Light cannot penetrate, but where the strangeness of bioluminescence is normal.

Let us harness our capacity to produce Light from within, similar to how the inscriptions on the walls of ancient temples where sunlight does not naturally reach, demonstrates for us the possibility and reality that Light travels in mysterious ways. As you read the following article, seek to acknowledge the various degrees I am addressing by my various statements and researches. See this as an exercise to identify your understanding and comprehension of the various perspectives presented above. This will prove fruitful to all who endeavor to complete this task, because it provides a subject upon which to exercise your developing gifts as a M.M. I interject some levity throughout the discourse, and also present my offerings in a way intentionally designed to confront the many loosely assembled counter-claims and arguments for my position. This is to purposely create discomfort and agitation, which will hopefully lead to an earnest seeking of more Light (similar to how sand agitating the mouth of an oyster produces a pearl). Without any further ado, with our evolved Masonic minds, let's get started.

The Two-Dollar-Bill Revisited

Jeff Menzise, Ph.D., 32°, FPS

*G*ood Brothers and Sistars, in order to further shed Light on a situation of seemingly great controversy, I have decided to take a trip down to the Bureau of Engraving & Printing in Washington, DC. My trip was for the sole purpose of better understanding the engraving and money printing process, in order to truly understand how the dark-faced man actually gets printed onto the two-dollar bill. I know many people believe that his presence has somehow been "debunked," and, therefore, is no longer worthy of discussion; however, I respectfully beg to differ. The amount of argument, and in some cases rage, and the attempts to suppress the discussion, brought about by my desire to revisit this topic, demonstrates the need for further exploration. If it has been proven, beyond a reasonable doubt, that there is in fact no representation of a "Black" man on the back of the two-dollar bill, then my further inquiry would simply be ignored; instead, it has stirred great emotion amongst some of the Brotherhood, specifically those who have taken a rather rigid stance on the topic. I am always will-ing and able to "agree-to-disagree," and definitely for the sake of maintaining peace and harmony. However, I am not willing to suppress my own God-given abilities to think and research for myself...this same, I strongly advise for all of my Brothers in the Craft.

In most of our institutions, we as American Africans tend to be behind the curve a bit. This, I believe is due to the fight and struggle we have had to endure, in order to be equal with our White counter-parts; this is true whether we are speaking of education and academic settings, work-place and employment, or the criminal justice system. The same holds true for our quest as Freemasons. From the initial petition submitted by the "Founding 15" of what was originally called the African Lodge, all the way to the present moment in which many are still seeking Recognition from "mainstream," or predominately White Masonic Grand Lodges and her member-ship, we have sought equality. Beyond recognition, we have also sought equality of resources, as well as, equality of Masonic understanding. Some have settled for the limited information, insights, and explana-tions that have been shared with us by our tried and true White Brothers, while others understand that there must be more Light to gain beyond their Esoteric, Historical, and Ritualistic offerings. This is similar to how when the "Founding 15" were Initiat-ed they could only perform funerals and march in procession; the information and abilities were severely limited. Thankfully, in their case, they were not satisfied with the restricted expression of Freemasonry, and thus, proceeded to gain more Light, seeking to express it to its fullest. I am cut from this same cloth.

Prior to being made aware that there were people who argued against the notion that there was a "Black" man on the back of the two-dollar-bill, I took it for granted that everyone saw the same thing that I saw. In fact, since this controversy has resurfaced, based on my writings, I have asked both college students, high school students, and elementary school students to look at the bill and tell me what they see. Invariably, 100% of the people shown this bill see the man with the dark face, each of them calling him a "Black man." As a professional and clinical researcher, I was sure not to bias their responses by giving a prompt other than, "Look at the faces on the back of this bill and tell me if you notice anything significant." I took this same precaution on my visit to the Bureau of Engraving and Printing (BEP).

While at the BEP, I took the tour that breezes its visitors past the actual printing plant and machines while the operators work. At our first stop, there was a GIANT two-dollar-bill rotating as it was suspended from the ceiling. There, as should be expected, was seated the same dark-faced man. As the tour guide discussed the machinery below us, she mentioned how EACH AND EVERY engraver, prior to being allowed to work for the Treasury and Bureau of Engraving, must complete a TEN-YEAR Apprenticeship. By the time they have completed their apprenticeship, they are Master Craftsmen and Master Craftswomen...tried and tested. This is significant because some have explained the dark-face to result from a mistake.

I asked the tour guide for more detail about the process but she was new, and thus could not provide me with more info but promised to get someone who could by the end of the tour. As we completed the 45-minute round, she met me in the gift shop with a Jewish Brother who was far more knowledgeable than she, in regards to the engraving process and the level of scrutiny given to every plate from which each bill is made.

The Brother, in response to my question: "How are the plates made to place ink on the bills?", described the process of cutting the Master plate with fine or coarse, deep or shallow grooves, all of which are designed to determine where the ink will actually be placed, and to what degree of darkness (from "black" to "white"). He explained everything from how much pressure the machines apply and even how they recently adjusted the master plates for the two-dollar bill in order to accommodate the new machinery, which applies more pressure and thus needs less ink, thereby using more shallow grooves for the darker portions of the image.

Here is the point of interest (although it was all interesting). I asked him specifically, "How are the darker places on the image made darker, and the lighter places made lighter?" He informed me that the Master Engravers cut deeper groves on the plate for the places that should hold ink, and therefore print ink onto the bill. The places that are meant to be darker, receive deeper grooves. In the case of faces, the "white" spaces receive little to no grooves... and the grooves that are cut, will invariably be shallow. On the other hand, the "darker" spaces receive more and deeper grooves.

Now that we were beyond the technical aspects of the process, I asked him plain and direct: "If there was a face that is colored in with dark ink, was that intentionally done?" He replied: "There are no mistakes on these bills. If it is on there, it was meant to be on there...these plates and every bill is thoroughly examined by many people. There is no way that a Master Plate will be cut out of specification. If the face is dark, it was meant to be dark."

He then asked what I was specifically speaking of, and I told him the two-dollar bill...he had never heard the "smear," "shadow," or even the "engraver's mistake" theories (all of which have been used by various "learned" people in an attempt to counter my claims). He assured me that if it was even possible of being a smear: 1) it wouldn't show up so consistently on every bill; 2) the fact that it does show up on every bill, the exact same way, means it was engraved with the full intention of showing up that way, and thus it is exactly as it is supposed to be.

In essence, he confirmed for those who still had a doubt, that the dark-faced man on the back of the two-dollar-bill is there by intention. Not by mistake, and not by happenstance, but by full intention. On a follow-up trip, this same employee asked his supervisor to come down and speak with me. We had a great conversation as well, actually looking at the two-dollar bill together (I typically carry and spend two-dollar bills); his response in full uninhibited amazement was "Wow, that sure does seem to be an image of a Black man sitting there."

True scholars will move on from the debate about whether it exists or not and will begin to seek to understand why it has been done. The so-called, "debunked myth," only deals with those who have speculated that he was Prince Hall, Benjamin Banneker, or someone else. That is not my fight. My position is, and has always been:

> ...based on the original painting, Robert Morris occupied that position. In the original painting, the artist's rendition is consistent with other images of the wealthy, former Senator and financier of the Revolutionary War; however, on the back of the two-dollar bill, it couldn't possibly be him. Why? Because he didn't have dark skin...shifting the argument to focus on the question: 'If it is a Black man,

then who is it?' That, we don't know. It may be no one in particular, It could simply be a symbolic representation of the Africans with whom the colonialists and some Founding Fathers had relationships and agreements (The Barbary Treaties 1786-1816 and the Treaty with Morocco). Remember, the scene painted is fictitious. There was never a time when everyone pictured, actually sat in the same room together. In fact, some of the images are based on relatives of the actual people featured because they were not available for the artist to draw from life...

On the other hand, a symbolist sees this very same image, complete with the position that this "dark-faced" person occupies (that of Robert Morris), and begins to wonder what could the symbolism of the name have to do with the symbolism of the image? Naturally, and obviously, there is a sign hidden in plain sight; the name Morris etymologically traces back to the word commonly used by Europeans for dark-skinned people, moor. As a symbolist, there is no need to deny the obvious to uphold certain 'facts' and positions; there is only a desire to seek the truth hidden behind the veil. As Freemasons, that is what we are taught, or at least told, to do.

<u>Symbolically Speaking, vol. 1</u> pp. xiv, xv

In the heat of one of these exchanges with several of our Brothers, I was reminded of the Richard Pryor joke where his wife catches him cheating with another woman. His punchline of the joke was, "Are you going to believe me or those lying eyes of yours?!" His point was to convince her that she was not seeing what she was seeing. In other words, trust what I tell you that you are looking at, and not what you know that you are seeing. The main counter-argument is that the vignette on the back of the two-dollar bill is based on Trumbull's portrait, and that this portrait did not include a "Black" man.

What many fail to realize is that there are two portraits by Trumbull, both depicting the presentation of the draft of the Declaration of Independence (many mistakenly believe this is an image of the actual signing of the Declaration of Independence). One such image, and perhaps the most popular version, is found in the Capitol Rotunda; the other, smaller and older version is found at Yale University. The irony is that even these two paintings differ from one another, including and omitting several people.

Even more ironic is the inclusion of two totally unknown characters on the master plate used to print the two-dollar bill. These two faces do not appear on the portrait's seating chart, and seem to literally appear out of nowhere. These facts are important because they show that the vignette used for the two-dollar bill is not an exact replica of the two portraits by Trumbull, and that the original engraver, Frederick Girsch, took creative license to deviate from the portrait, and that the subsequent engravers: Edward M. Hall, Edward E. Myers, George Frederick Cumming Smillie, Joachim Benzing, and Frank Lamasure (1915 version); and Edward P. Archer, Kenneth Wiram, and Albert Saavedra (1976 version used for the two-dollar bill) all maintained Girsch's deviations from the original portraits.

Some have written to the BEP seeking clarity regarding this mysterious man appearing on the back of the two-dollar bill. The BEP has issued letters, two of which I have read, basically stating that there is no "black" man on the two-dollar bill, and that the dark face of Robert Morris is simply due to the amount of detail given to the image.

In light of what I have presented in this lecture, this explanation seems to contradict the factual information regarding the engraving process. The only way the face becomes dark, is for the engravers to cut a groove in the plate to hold and thus impress ink onto the bill. If Robert Morris' face were to remain "white," there would be no need for any detail, it would simply be left alone, or cut with the shallowest of grooves. Instead, these Master Engravers have all dug deep into the master plate, ensuring that the entire face of Robert Morris would be colored-in darker than anyone else's on the vignette; even those that are literally standing in the shadows, and whose faces are literally cloaked in a shadow on the portrait.

Another point about the letters received from the BEP by certain inquirers, is that the word "black" is written in quotation marks. I find this interesting and see that it could literally mean that there is no man with black-colored-ink on the back of the bill, which is an absolutely true statement. There aren't any "white" men there either; only shades of green.

Until this mystery is finally solved, I suggest that every Brother of the Craft go to their bank and get themselves a few two-dollar bills. Keep them with your other relics and periodically take a look at the man seated at the table behind and over the right shoulders of the drafting committee (these are the five men standing facing the table where John Hancock is seated in the foreground). While examining this bill, ask yourself, are you going to believe the nay-sayers, or your own "lying" eyes?

Other Mind on the Matter Publications

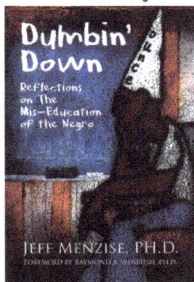

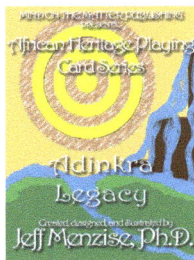

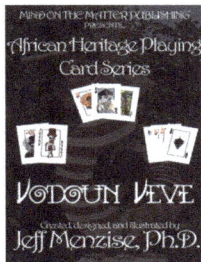

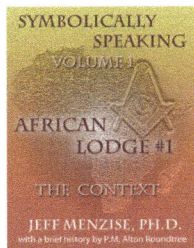

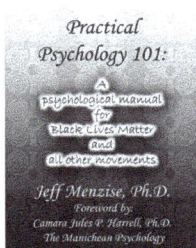

Dumbin' Down
Reflections on The Mis-Education of the Negro

JEFF MENZISE, PH.D.
FOREWORD BY RAYMOND A. WINBUSH, PH.D.

J. A. Rogers
RAMBLING RUMINATIONS
RARE WRITINGS FROM THE COLLECTION OF JOEL AUGUSTUS ROGERS

COMPILED AND EDITED BY JEFF MENZISE, PH.D.
FOREWORD BY MOLEFI K. ASANTE, PH.D.

MIND ON THE MATTER PUBLISHING PRESENTS...
African Heritage Playing Card Series
Adinkra Legacy
Created, designed and illustrated by Jeff Menzise, Ph.D.

MIND ON THE MATTER PUBLISHING PRESENTS...
African Heritage Playing Card Series
VODOUN VEVE
Created, designed and illustrated by Jeff Menzise, Ph.D.

SYMBOLICALLY SPEAKING
VOLUME 1
AFRICAN LODGE #1
THE CONTEXT
JEFF MENZISE, PH.D.
with a brief history by P.M. Alton Roundtree

Practical Psychology 101:
A psychological manual for Black Lives Matter and all other movements
Jeff Menzise, Ph.D.
Foreword by Camara Jules P. Harrell, Ph.D.
The Manichean Psychology